How to use these questions

- These questions are made for adult learners.

- Give one set of questions to a pair. One student asks the other answers.
- The students answering can deflect the question by asking 'How about you?'

- Students can also work in threes.

- Have them switch roles halfway through.

- Students should answer in a complete sentence as much as possible.

- Keep in mind the one asking the questions is also practicing English.

- The questions are designed for all levels.

- Beginners should start learning idioms right away. After all, idioms are just normal everyday English. The sooner they learn it, the better. The student doesn't need to know it's an idiom. They just need to know the meaning.

- The questions are not chosen randomly. The questions themselves, apart from the possible answers, have something to teach. It might be a new word or a sentence structure.

- I will ask a student whom I know doesn't have a car "Where did you buy your car?'. I will do this in order to teach: 'I don't have one.' Or I throw in a question that I know cannot be answered, for example, 'What is the BBGHJ theory?' I do this to teach a response such as 'Beats me!' or "Search me!' Furthermore, there might be a question with an obvious answer, but the point is for the student to practice a structure by responding in a complete sentence. For example:

  Student A: How do people in your country celebrate birthdays?
  Student B: Party
  Teacher: Answer in a complete sentence.
  Student B: We have parties.

  As a result, the student practices *have a party*.

- These questions also serve as a good warm up for a new topic that will be introduced either in discussion, listening or reading. I find it works better when students work in pairs or small groups.

1

TABLE OF CONTENTS

ADVICE

1. What advice would you give to someone who wants to stop smoking?

2. What advice would you give to someone in debt?

3. What advice would you give to someone whose partner is cheating on him/her?

4. What advice would you give to someone who is trying to decide whether to go to college or not?

5. What advice would you give to someone who wants to learn another language?

6. What advice would you give to someone who wants to visit your country?

7. What suggestions do you have for someone who wants to get fit?

8. Do you have any recommendations for a good place to grab a bite?

9. What advice do you have for someone who has noisy neighbors?

10. Where do you go to get good advice?

11. What advice would you give someone who wants to make more money?

12. What do you say to someone who is homesick?

13. I found a wallet with 300 bucks and a driver's license. What should I do?

14. My roommates are very messy. What should I do?

15. How can I make new friends in this city?

16. I want to buy a new computer. Do you have any suggestions?

17. I want to find a good podcast. What do you suggest?

18. I want to get a better cell phone plan. What do you suggest?

19. Have you ever gotten a bad piece of advice?

20. Whose advice do you follow more, that of your parents or that of your friends?

21. I need to choose between the TOEFL and IELTS. What should I do?

22. I want to cut down on social media. What should I do?

AGE

1. Would you like to live to a ripe old age?

2. At what age can you get a driver's license?

3. At what age should one get married?

4. What's the average life expectancy in your country?

5. At what age are you over the hill?

6. In your country, who takes care of ageing parents?

7. In your country, are senior citizens active?

8. What is the generation gap?

9. Are your grandparents still alive?

10. Are your great-grandparents still alive?

11. How old do you have to be to vote?

12. How old do you have to be to drink?

13. At what age do people retire?

14. Are there any benefits to old age?

15. What are the drawbacks to old age?

16. In what countries is the population ageing?

17. What's the best age?

18. What's age discrimination?

19. Should older people save their money for their children or spend it on themselves?

20. Are older people wiser? Why or why not?

21. What's the best age to learn a language?

22. Where do you want to live when you get old?

ANNOYANCES

1. What annoys you about where you live now?

2. What are some things we love to hate?

3. What's your pet peeve?

4. What are some common pet peeves?

5. What do you think about slow walkers?

6. What do you think about noisy eaters?

7. What do you think about people who talk loudly on the phone?

8. What do you think about people who tap, fidget and bounce knees?

9. Does it bother you when you're talking to someone and they won't stop staring at their phone screen?

10. Does it bother you when you're in a public bathroom but there is no toilet paper in the stall?

11. Does it bother you when people bite their nails?

12. Does it bother you when people interrupt you when you are speaking?

13. Does it bug you when you have to repeat yourself multiple times?

14. Does it bug you when a computer or phone won't load a page fast enough?

15. Does it drive you crazy when you have to deal with a lot of red tape?

16. What do you think about people who suck at a straw until it makes a slurping sound?

17. Does it bug you when someone leaves the light on in a room that isn't being used?

18. Does it bug you when people sneeze or cough without covering their mouths?

19. Does getting gum on your shoe irritate you?

20. Do know-it-alls drive you up the wall?

21. Does it bug you when people make a lot of noise when they are chewing gum?

BODY LANGUAGE

1. What is body language?

2. In your country, how do you signal somebody to come here?

3. Is body language more honest than spoken language?

4. How do you make a great first impression?

5. What is the most attractive type of body language?

6. What message do you send when you cross your arms?

7. What message do you send when you talk to someone standing sideways?

8. What does it mean when you twirl your hair?

9. Do all cultures have the same body language?

10. What does it mean when you clasp your hands behind your back?

11. How do you signal a waiter in your country?

12. Using your face and body only, how do you say:

13. -I'm bored.
14. -disgusting
15. -I don't know.
16. -crazy
17. -good idea
18. -the best
19. -I'm embarrassed.
20. -I don't want to talk to you.
21. -I'm nervous.

22. What gesture do you use when you want to say hello to someone?

23. What gesture do you use when something's delicious?

24. What gesture do you use when you talk about money?

25. Is it polite to point at people?

26. Do you maintain eye contact when you talk to people?

BUSINESS

1. Do you run your own business?

2. Is there a specific company you would like t work for?

3. What's the difference between a co-worker and a colleague?

4. What are some companies that have bad reputations?

5. Can you think of any companies well known for their exceptional customer service?

6. What is a monopoly?

7. What is an internship program?

8. What are the pros and cons of being an entrepreneur?

9. Would you rather work for a big company or a small company?

10. What's the economic forecast for this year?

11. When is a company in the red?

12. What can businesses do to succeed?

13. Have you ever worked in retail?

14. Do you see yourself working a 9 to5 the rest of your life?

15. How do you feel about job interviews?

16. Are you good at negotiating?

17. What are some good negotiating strategies?

18. Are you willing to work abroad?

19. What is proper business attire?

20. If someone gets the pink slip, what should they do?

21. Are you good at crunching numbers?

22. Do businesses in your country have to deal with a lot of government red tape?

CARS AND DRIVING

1. How long have you had your driver's license?

2. What kind of cars do you like?

3. Have you ever driven a lemon?

4. What do you keep in the glove compartment of your car?

5. Do you know how to change a flat?

6. Why is it always a bad idea to thumb a ride?

7. Do you belong to AAA?

8. What's your favorite means of transportation?

9. What should you do if you get pulled over by the cops?

10. Do you know how to jump start a car?

11. Can you drive a stick?

12. Do you drive a hard bargain?

13. How many speeding tickets have you gotten?

14. Have you ever been the victim of road rage?

15. What kind of motorcycle do you have?

16. Where did you drive yesterday?

17. Where did you buy your last car?

18. Are you a backseat driver?

19. Are you a good driver?

20. Has your car ever broken down?

21. What's the speed limit in your country?

22. Can you drive a stick?

CHILDHOOD

1. Where did you grow up?

2. What games did you play?

3. Who was your best friend?

4. Did you have a lot of toys?

5. Did your parents punish you if you did something bad?

6. Were you a good student?

7. How old were you when you learned how to ride a bike?

8. Did you play outside a lot?

9. How late did you stay out?

10. Do you wish you could go back to being a kid?

11. What did you want to be when you grew up?

12. Do you have fond memories of your childhood?

13. Did you share a room with any of your siblings?

14. Which siblings were you the closest with?

15. Which siblings did you quarrel the most with?

16. Did you have a lot of chores?

17. Did your family sit together at mealtime?

18. Did you have any pets?

19. What was your favorite food growing up?

20. Were you a picky eater?

21. How many times did you move as a child?

22. Did your parents give you an allowance?

CITIES

1. You are travelling to a new city. Ask someone who knows the city

2. -how/airport/downtown?
3. -good place/stay?
4. -transportation in the city?
5. -places/eat?

6. Have you ever been to Brussels?

7. Have you ever been to Chicago?

8. What city would you like to live in?

9. What's the most expensive city in the world?

10. What's your least favorite city?

11. Why is more of the world's population moving to cities?

12. What cities would you like to visit?

13. How will cities change in the future?

14. What city is known for fashion?

15. What city is known for finance?

16. What city is known for food?

17. What city has excelled in terms of innovation?

18. Does your city have a lot of high-rises?

19. What makes a city thrive?

20. What makes a city livable?

21. What aspects of a city do people complain about?

22. What cities are threatened by rising sea levels?

23. If you could change one thing about your city, what would it be?

24. What is a sister city?

CLOTHES/FASHION

1. What do you have on?

2. Do you follow fashion?

3. What do you think about piercings?

4. Do you think men should be allowed to wear skirts?

5. Do you have any tattoos?

6. Would you ever dye your hair? If so, what color?

7. How should you dress for an interview?

8. What do you think of casual Fridays?

9. Would you ever wear sandals to work?

10. What colors look good on you?

11. What styles are popular now?

12. What's your favorite clothing store?

13. Do you like to buy clothes online?

14. Are there any drawbacks to buying clothes online?

15. Do you like baggy clothes?

16. Do you wear shorts?

17. Do you always try on clothes before you buy them?

18. Do you like to wear brand clothing?

19. Do you always hang on to your receipts after you buy something?

20. Do you ever buy secondhand clothing?

21. Are you fashion conscious?

22. Have you ever worn a piece of clothing inside out?

COLD

1. Are you chilly?

2. Do you like winter?

3. Have you ever gone skiing?

4. How long does it take to get over a cold?

5. Have you ever gotten cold feet?

6. When was the last time somebody gave you the cold shoulder?

7. Has anybody been cold-hearted to you?

8. Why would somebody go cold turkey?

9. How often do you catch colds?

10. Have you ever made a cold call?

11. Do you agree that revenge is a dish best served cold?

12. Are you going to chill out this weekend?

13. In what situation would somebody tell you to freeze?

14. Are you snowed under at work?

15. What's the difference between 'cool' and 'cold'?

16. What's a good way to break the ice with someone?

17. Do you ever leave your family out in the cold on what is happening in your life?

18. Have you ever tried cross-country skiing?

19. What is a blizzard?

20. Have you ever gotten frostbite?

21. Is your house drafty (draughty)?

22. Do you like to shovel (snow)?

COOKING

1. Do you know how to cook?

2. Do you like to cook?

3. What do you have in your kitchen?

4. Do you eat in the kitchen?

5. Do you cook breakfast?

6. Do you like to make dinner for your friends?

7. What are your favorite recipes?

8. Do you have any secret recipes?

9. What is a staple food in your country?

10. What are popular ways in your country to make vegetables and meat?

11. Do you use a peeler to peel potatoes?

12. Do you have a spatula in your kitchen?

13. How many an openers do you have?

14. How do you make eggs?

15. Do you have a grater?

16. Do you steam broccoli?

17. Do you have a carving knife? What do you carve?

18. How do I know that I'm cooking rice correctly?

19. Why is rolling out pizza dough so difficult?

20. How do you keep pasta from clumping?

21. How do you keep from crying when cutting onions?

22. How do you know if eggs are fresh?

CRIME

1. Is there a lot of crime in your country?

2. What kind of crime is most prevalent?

3. Does your country have capital punishment?

4. Have you ever been mugged?

5. What is a home invasion?

6. Have you ever been carjacked?

7. What's the punishment for shoplifting in your country?

8. Are there a lot of pickpockets in your hometown?

9. Have you ever had anything stolen from you?

10. How can you protect yourself from crime?

11. Is the crime rate increasing?

12. Does your hometown have gangs?

13. What is vandalism?

14. Have you ever witnessed a crime?

15. Do police solve most crimes?

16. What is an alibi?

17. What does a detective do?

18. What is a cold case?

19. What is domestic violence?

20. What is a juvenile?

21. Do you have good street smarts?

22. How can we avoid crime when we are traveling?

DECISIONS

1. Do you usually make decisions quickly or do you need to sleep on it?

2. Is being decisive a good quality?

3. Tell me about a time when you had to choose the lesser of two evils.

4. What decisions have you made about your future?

5. Do you have a plan B?

6. Do you like to test the waters before making a solid commitment?

7. Are you torn between choosing a job you love versus a job that makes good money?

8. Do you often make mountains out of molehills?

9. Are you good at making decisions?

10. What process do you follow when making a decision?

11. Tell me about a time when you had to make an immediate decision on a critical issue.

12. Have you ever been advised to go with your gut?

13. Do you have good intuition?

14. Have you ever regretted making a decision?

15. Do you like to keep your options open?

16. Who calls the shots in your family?

17. Why is it difficult for some people to make up their minds?

18. What are some important decisions people make in their lives?

19. Is it important to get other people's input before making a workplace decision?

20. Have you ever been between a rock and a hard place?

21. Is being indecisive a sign of anxiety?

THE ENVIRONMENT

1. What is the environment?

2. Is the environment in trouble?

3. What can we do to help the environment?

4. Do you recycle?

5. Are you a litterbug?

6. What is pollution?

7. What are the main types of waste?

8. What can we do to improve air quality?

9. Is the tap water in your home safe to drink?

10. What is alternative energy?

11. Explain the process of global warming.

12. Does secondhand smoke hurt the environment?

13. How will climate change affect the world?

14. Is the amount of snow and ice on earth decreasing?

15. What is eutrophication?

16. Besides mercury, what other heavy metals cause pollution?

17. What natural landscapes have the most appeal to you?

18. Do you like the sound of wind rustling the leaves?

19. Why do trees have sap?

20. What is deforestation?

21. What lives in hollow logs?

22. What is biodiversity?

FAMILY

1. How big is your family?

2. What is a nuclear family?

3. What is an extended family?

4. In your country, until what age do people live with their parents?

5. How many cousins do you have?

6. Who is the breadwinner in your family?

7. Do you come from a close-knit family?

8. How many siblings do you have?

9. Do you get along with your siblings?

10. Did your older brother pick on you when you were a kid?

11. Is blood thicker than water?

12. Are your great-grandparents still alive?

13. What is a foster family?

14. What's the best thing about family?

15. What is your favorite family tradition?

16. What are the most important qualities in a good parent?

17. Do you take after anyone in your family?

18. Do you enjoy family get-togethers?

19. Do you always see eye to eye with your family?

20. Are you a chip off the old block?

21. Does anything run in your family?

22. Would you like to start a family?

FEARS

1. Are you afraid of spiders?

2. Are you afraid of snakes?

3. Are you afraid of cockroaches?

4. Are you afraid of needles?

5. Are you afraid of ghosts?

6. What are you afraid of?

7. Do you know anyone with a phobia?

8. Are you afraid of heights?

9. Is it true that the only thing we need to fear is fear itself?

10. What is the number one fear in America?

11. Are you afraid of going to the dentist or doctor?

12. Are you afraid of giving a speaking presentation?

13. How can one overcome fear?

14. Do some people fear success?

15. Why are most people afraid to make mistakes?

16. Are you afraid of flying?

17. Have you ever been scared stiff?

18. What freaks you out?

19. Does the sound of thunder send chills down your spine?

20. Do you like horror movies?

21. Do you have nerves of steel?

22. Are you frightened of the future?

FESTIVALS/HOLIDAYS

1. What's your favorite holiday?

2. What's the biggest holiday in your country?

3. What's the difference between a festival and a holiday?

4. What is a feast?

5. In your country, on which holidays do people give gifts?

6. Do you think there should be more holidays?

7. Is there a spring festival in your country?

8. What are some summer holidays?

9. Is there an autumn 'harvest' festival in your country?

10. What are some winter holidays?

11. Are there any holidays associated with cookouts?

12. What's the strangest festival that you have heard of?

13. Would you rather be a kid or a grandparent during the holidays?

14. Why do we have holidays?

15. Who do you like to go to festivals with?

16. Have you ever been to a parade?

17. What are some special foods you cook for festivals?

18. What is the famous celebration in Rio de Janeiro?

19. What is Oktoberfest?

20. What is the Burning Man festival?

21. Have you ever been to the running of the bulls?

22. If you could create a festival, what would it be?

FOOD

1. Do you have a big appetite?

2. What do you usually have for breakfast?

3. What do you usually have for lunch?

4. What do you usually have for dinner?

5. Do you have a sweet tooth?

6. Would some good food put you in a good mood?

7. Do you usually have seconds?

8. What kind of poultry do you eat?

9. Do you like green beans?

10. Do you like black beans?

11. Do you like white beans?

12. Do you like human beings?

13. How often do you eat out?

14. Do you like spicy food?

15. Would you rather eat out or eat at home?

16. Do you eat like a bird or a horse?

17. What produce do you buy?

18. Are your eyes bigger than your belly?

19. Do you eat junk food?

20. Would you like to grab a bite after class?

21. Do you eat between meals?

22. Do you know how to cook?

FUTURE/PREDICTIONS

1. What will the world be like twenty years from now?

2. What will the world be like 500 years from now?

3. What will computers be like ten years from now?

4. Will time travel be possible?

5. Will there be more natural disasters?

6. Will people still have cell phones?

7. Will most animals be extinct?

8. What will the average life expectancy be?

9. Will human cloning be commonplace?

10. Will borders between countries disappear?

11. Will houses be bigger or smaller?

12. Will Facebook still be around in the future?

13. Where do you see yourself in the long run?

14. Will we discover life on other planets?

15. What will be the main source of energy when oil reserves are depleted?

16. Will humans colonize another planet?

17. Will we put computers in human bodies?

18. Will AI be commonplace?

19. How will healthcare change?

20. How much will the human population increase in the future?

21. What will fashion be like?

22. Are you looking forward to the future?

HABITS

1. Can you name ten bad habits?

2. How can you kick a bad habit?

3. What are ten good habits?

4. How can you develop good habits?

5. Which bad habit is the hardest to get rid of?

6. What are some healthy eating habits?

7. Do you bite your nails?

8. How can we form a new positive habit and stick with it?

9. Why do people willingly engage in self-destructive habits?

10. "We are what we repeatedly do. Excellence, then, is not an act, but a habit." – **Aristotle**-Do you agree or disagree with that statement?

11. Is happiness a habit?

12. What are some habits that really bug you?

13. Are you a couch potato?

14. Is skipping breakfast a bad habit?

15. Where do we pick up our habits?

16. What are some bad habits children have?

17. Is procrastination a habit?

18. What are some odd habits that you've heard about?

19. Would you break up with your partner because of a bad habit?

20. What are some good study habits?

21. Do you like routines or do you like to do things on the spur of the moment?

22. Are you a creature of habit?

HEALTH/ILLNESS

1. Do you have a headache?

2. Do you have a backache?

3. Do you have a stomachache?

4. Do you have a toothache?

5. Do you have chocolate cake?

6. Does your knee hurt?

7. Do you take vitamins?

8. How long does it take to get over a cold?

9. Do you have any allergies?

10. What do you do when you get the hiccups?

11. Have you ever passed out?

12. Are you feeling under the weather?

13. What would you say to someone who is recovering from surgery?

14. What do you do for an upset stomach?

15. How often do you get sick?

16. What's the matter? Are you feeling OK?

17. Did you make an appointment with the doctor?

18. What do you take for a headache?

19. Do you think prevention is the best cure?

20. What's your blood type?

21. Would you like to be a nurse?

22. Are you afraid of needles?

HOUSING

1. What city do you live in?

2. What street do you live on?

3. What kind of house do you have?

4. How many floors does your house have?

5. Does your house have a yard?

6. Does your house have a garage?

7. Do you live in a house or an apartment?

8. What floor do you live on?

9. Do you have smoke detectors in your house?

10. Do you rent or own?

11. What's your zip code?

12. Do you live in a condo?

13. Who does the decorating in your house?

14. Do you have a driveway?

15. Is your house in a convenient location?

16. What do you like most about your place?

17. What do you like least about your place?

18. Where would you like to live?

19. Where do you park?

20. How long have you lived in your place?

21. If you could change anything about your place, what would it be?

22. What's the most expensive city to live in?

HOW OFTEN

1. How often do you go dancing?

2. How often do you go swimming?

3. How often do you go jogging?

4. How often do you go camping?

5. How often do you go shopping?

6. How often do you iron?

7. How often do you cook?

8. How often do you stay up late?

9. How often do you go to the theater?

10. How often do you travel?

11. How often do you read?

12. How often do you take public transportation?

13. How often do you eat pizza?

14. How often do you eat ice-cream?

15. How often do you get take-out food?

16. How often do you do laundry?

17. How often do you check your email?

18. How often does it rain in your hometown?

19. How often does it snow in your hometown?

20. How often do you go food shopping?

21. How often do you eat chocolate?

22. How often did you get in trouble when you were a kid?

JOB SEARCH

1. What kind of job are you looking for?

2. What kind of qualifications do you need for that job?

3. Do you have the skills you need for that job? If not what can you do?

4. What online resources do you use when job hunting?

5. Is the field that you want to work in competitive?

6. Do you have a resume/CV?

7. How long should your resume/CV be?

8. What skills are impressive to have on a resume?

9. When reading a resume, what red flags do recruiters look out for?

10. Should you go to the employer's place and drop off my resume?

11. If you keep sending out resumes, but don't get any interviews. What can you do?

12. What's appropriate attire for a job interview?

13. What are some common interview questions?

14. How should you respond to, "What's your biggest weakness?"

15. How should you respond when someone asks what your salary expectations are?

16. What are some common interview mistakes?

17. What questions should you ask in an interview?

18. This is a catch-22: You need experience to get a job, but you need a job to get experience. What can you do?

19. How do you keep up your morale during a job hunt?

20. Where are you searching for job leads (besides the job boards)?

21. Are you using social media?

22. How far are you willing to commute for a new job?

MANNERS

What are some good manners?

What are some good table manners?

What are some bad manners?

What are some bad manners regarding the use of cell phones?

What are some bad manners drivers have?

What is proper etiquette when riding an elevator?

Did people have better manners in the past?

Do you greet strangers on the street?

Is it good manners to tuck in your shirt?

What manners were you taught as a kid?

Is it rude to stare at someone?

Is it rude to point at someone?

Is it impolite to yawn in public?

Is it acceptable to burp while eating?

Is it rude to get on a train before others have gotten off?

Is it OK to eavesdrop on other people's conversations?

Is it bad manners to comb or brush your hair in public?

Is it OK to ignore an RSVP request?

What do you think about using foul language?

What do you think about texting in movie theaters?

Is it good manners to ask to be excused before leaving the dinner table?

Is it good manners to stand up when a senior enters the room?

LIFE

1. Where were you born?

2. Where did you grow up?

3. Where did you go to high school?

4. What was your favorite subject in high school?

5. Did you go to college?

6. Are you going to college?

7. When did you graduate from high school? College?

8. Where did you go on your honeymoon?

9. How many kids do you have?

10. What do you do?

11. How long have you been married?

12. Where is your spouse from?

13. Did you get divorced?

14. Are you retired?

15. When would you like to retire?

16. What's your hometown?

17. Do you get homesick?

18. Did you study English in your hometown?

19. How many siblings do you have?

20. Do you get along with your in-laws?

21. Where do you see yourself five years from now?

22. How do you like this city?

MARRIAGE

1. How long have you been married?

2. What are the pros and cons of being married?

3. Where did you go on your honeymoon?

4. What is the secret to a happy marriage?

5. Do you get along well with your in-laws?

6. Where did you meet your spouse?

7. Do your parents want you to settle down?

8. What are some reasons that people get divorced?

9. Do you know anyone who has had an arranged marriage?

10. Does marriage mean giving up freedom?

11. Should a husband and wife split the household chores?

12. Do you think you have to marry someone of the same religion?

13. Does your spouse point out your flaws?

14. What are the qualities of a good husband?

15. Is marriage for life?

16. Would you get divorced if you could marry your favorite celebrity?

17. Are you ready to tie the knot?

18. What is the purpose of marriage?

19. What is the best way to handle disagreements in a marriage?

20. Would you share all money with your spouse or split the money into different accounts?

21. How do you think your life would change if you got married?

22. Do you believe love can pull you through anything?

MEDICINE/
PHARMACIES/REMEDIES

1. What do you do?

2. Where were you born?

3. Whereabouts?

4. What is a prescription drug?

5. What is an over- the- counter drug?

6. What do you know about the medicinal value of plants?

7. What can you feel on your neck or wrist as you heart pumps blood through your arteries?

8. What part of a plant grows underground?

9. Would you like to be a pharmacist?

10. What's the starting salary for a pharmacist?

11. Where do you get your prescriptions filled?

12. Why can't we read doctor's handwriting?

13. How can you quell nausea?

14. How can you treat a cold?

15. How can you get rid of the hiccups?

16. What's a good remedy for heartburn?

17. What's a good remedy for a headache?

18. How do you treat a stomachache?

19. How do you treat a bee sting?

20. Do you know any homemade hair treatments?

21. What plants have healing powers?

MEETING SOMEONE

1. What's your name?

2. Where do you come from?

3. How long have you been here?

4. What do you do?

5. How do you spend your **free** time?

6. Where do you live?

7. What are you into?

8. Are you married?

9. Do you have kids?

10. Do you come from a big family?

11. Why are you studying English?

12. Have you ever lived in another country?

13. Do you speak any other languages?

14. At what time of day are you at your best?

15. Where do you see yourself in the long run?

16. How do you come to school?

17. How long does it take?

18. What kind of food do you like?

19. Do you work out?

20. Do you ever get homesick?

21. Would you like to grab a bite some time?

22. What are some good places to visit in your country?

MONEY

1. Are you good at saving money?

2. Are you a big spender or a penny pincher?

3. How much money do you have on you now?

4. Why do some people have trouble making ends meet?

5. What advice would you give to someone in debt?

6. Do you make a budget at the end of every month?

7. Name the U.S. coins.

8. Can you spare a quarter?

9. Can you spare a buck?

10. Is money important?

11. Are we moving towards a cashless society?

12. Can you lend me five bucks?

13. What's the most expensive city in the world?

14. What kind of bank accounts are there?

15. How much does a new car cost?

16. Do you have any loose change?

17. How much does a new car go for?

18. If you had to choose between money or love, which would you choose?

19. Do you know your credit score?

20. Are you rolling in dough, or are you broke?

21. What would you do if you won the lottery?

22. How much do you have on you right now?

MOVIES

1. What kind of movies do you like?

2. How often do you go to the movies?

3. How much does a movie cost these days?

4. Where do you like to sit when you go to the movies?

5. Do you buy popcorn or any other snacks?

6. Do you like 3D movies?

7. Do you ever go to the movies alone?

8. Does it bug you when people text or talk during the movie?

9. What are some of your favorite movies?

10. Do you like horror movies?

11. What movie theater do you usually go to?

12. Do you ever go to the movies on a weekday?

13. Would you rather go to the movies or watch one at home?

14. What are the pros of watching a movie at home?

15. Who are your favorite actors?

16. Would you rather read or watch a movie?

17. Would you like to be a movie extra?

18. Would you like to be a celebrity?

19. What's the difference between 'see' a movie and 'watch' a movie?

20. Have you ever seen two movies in a row?

21. What's the worst movie you've ever seen?

22. Do you like foreign films?

NATURAL DISASTERS

1. Have you ever been in a natural disaster?

2. Have you ever experienced an earthquake?

3. Have you ever experienced a mudslide?

4. Are there mudslides in your country?

5. Are there wildfires in your country?

6. Have you ever experienced a drought?

7. Would you like to be a firefighter?

8. Have you ever been in a blizzard?

9. Have you ever experienced a hurricane?

10. Are there hurricanes in your country?

11. Have you ever seen a tornado?

12. Have you ever experienced a tidal wave?

13. Have you ever experienced a flood?

14. Have you ever been part of a search and rescue team?

15. What natural disasters occur in your country?

16. What can you do to prepare for a natural disaster?

17. What is the emergency phone number in your country?

18. What organizations help you in an emergency?

19. What natural disasters have happened recently?

20. Are natural disasters happening more frequently?

21. What natural disaster are you most afraid of?

22. What is worse, a natural disaster or a manmade disaster?

NUMBERS

1. Do you have a lucky number?

2. What's the population of your country?

3. What's 2+2?

4. What's 2+2-1?

5. What's 20/4?

6. What's 2 x 10?

7. How many are in a dozen?

8. Are you good at math?

9. Are you on cloud nine?

10. Are you a good dancer or do you have two left feet?

11. What jobs require you to be good with numbers?

12. Would you consider becoming an accountant?

13. Are there any numbers that are considered unlucky in your culture?

14. Are there any numbers that are considered lucky in your culture?

15. Are you good with numbers?

16. Can you count backwards subtracting seven every time?

17. Is math important in daily life? How come?

18. Do you know how to read Roman numerals?

19. What century is this?

20. What is the area of a circle?

21. In a fraction, what is the denominator?

22. What are even and odd numbers?

PARENTING/KIDS

1. Where did you grow up?

2. What was your childhood like?

3. What were you like in high school?

4. Where is a good place to raise kids?

5. Whom do you kids take after more, you or your spouse?

6. Do you spoil your kids?

7. Is it OK to spank kids?

8. At what age is it appropriate for a kid to get a cell phone?

9. What's your opinion on vaccinations?

10. Are your kids picky eaters?

11. Are kids these days different from previous generations?

12. How many kids would you like to have?

13. Is it easy to raise a kid?

14. Did you rebel against your parents?

15. Did your parents give you a curfew when you were a kid?

16. Did your parents give you an allowance?

17. Did you have to do a lot of chores when you were a kid?

18. Did you get into mischief?

19. Were your parents strict?

20. When you were a kid, did your family sit together at every meal?

21. What did you talk about at the dinner table?

22. Who was your favorite babysitter?

PEOPLE/RELATIONSHIPS

1. Who(m) do you look up to?

2. Do you get along with your siblings?

3. How often do your in-laws visit?

4. Are Facebook friends real friends?

5. Is there a friend limit on Facebook?

6. Did you older brother or sister pick on you when you were a kid?

7. How often do you get together with friends?

8. How do you keep in touch with your family members?

9. Are you a social butterfly?

10. Does it worry you that kids spend too much time staring at screens rather than playing?

11. Would you rather have a few close friends or a lot of superficial ones?

12. Do you get along with your co-workers?

13. Do you come from a tight-knit family?

14. What king of people do you like?

15. What kind of people drive you up the wall?

16. Are you a people person?

17. Would you give the shirt off your back to help a friend?

18. Do you always see eye to eye with your spouse?

19. Do you remember a time when you started off on the wrong foot with somebody?

20. What are the qualities of a good friend?

21. What are the qualities of a good boss?

22. What kind of person is a know-it-all?

RESTAURANTS

1. How often do you eat out?

2. Where is a good place around here to grab a bite?

3. Do you tip in your country?

4. When you eat out, do you usually get an appetizer?

5. If you went on a date, what kind of restaurant would you go to?

6. Do you usually get dessert?

7. What are you favorite desserts?

8. When a couple goes out on a date, which should pick up the tab?

9. Have you ever worked in a restaurant?

10. How do you like your steak?

11. What's the best restaurant you have been to?

12. What restaurant would you like to go to?

13. What kind of food do you like?

14. Do you ever go to buffets?

15. Have you ever had a bad experience eating out?

16. What's the difference between eating out and eating outside?

17. Do you ever take food home in a doggie bag?

18. When you eat a nice meal, what do you wash it down with?

19. Would you send food back if it didn't taste look good?

20. What is an early bird special?

21. Would you ever want to be a restaurant critic?

22. What makes a good restaurant location?

SCHOOL/STUDYING

1. What time does school start?

2. How many breaks do you have?

3. How long are your breaks?

4. What do you do for lunch?

5. What time do you get out of school?

6. Do you like school?

7. How often do you burn the midnight oil?

8. What are the qualities of a good student?

9. What's your favorite subject?

10. Have you got a pen I can borrow?

11. How often do you hit the books?

12. If you could study at any school in the world, where would you study?

13. What do you think about the rising cost of tuition?

14. What do you think about homeschooling?

15. What are the qualities of a good teacher?

16. Would you rather study alone or in a group?

17. What time do you get out of school?

18. Did you wear a uniform in school? If so, what did you think about it?

19. How do you get to school?

20. Do you ever cut class?

21. When you were a kid, did you like school?

22. Are you still in touch with your high school classmates?

THE SENSES

1. Name the five senses.

2. Do you have a sixth sense?

3. Are you hard of hearing?

4. Which of your senses is the sharpest?

5. How does strong unsweetened coffee taste?

6. Do you have good eyesight?

7. What are your favorite flavors?

8. Do you have a good sense of smell?

9. Do you like the smell of coffee?

10. Do you like the smell of cinnamon?

11. Which part of the brain processes smell?

12. How do our taste buds work?

13. What is the maximum frequency a human ear can hear?

14. Do you have ESP?

15. How would our world change if we had new and different senses?

16. What is common sense?

17. Are animal senses better than human senses?

18. How can you sharpen your senses?

19. What is nearsightedness? What about farsightedness?

20. Which parts of your body do you use for each of the five senses?

21. Is intuition an extra sense?

22. What part of the ear provides equilibrium?

SHOPPING

1. Do you like to shop?

2. What are you favorite stores?

3. What was the last thing you got that was on sale?

4. Do you hang on to your receipts?

5. Are you a bargain hunter?

6. What kind of stuff do you buy online?

7. What kind of stuff do you buy in stores?

8. Do you haggle?

9. What's the difference between 'for sale' and 'on sale'?

10. Do you count your change after you buy something?

11. Do you like shopping for clothes?

12. Do you always try on clothes before you buy them?

13. What do you have on your wish list?

14. Is shopping a hobby for some people?

15. Are you a shopaholic?

16. Would you rather go shopping alone or with friends?

17. Do you ever go on shopping sprees?

18. Do you like shopping malls?

19. Do women like shopping more than men?

20. Have you ever stood in line to buy a popular item before the store opened?

21. Have you ever worked in retail?

22. Do you participate in any loyalty programs?

SLEEP

1. How many hours sleep a night do you get?

2. Are you a light sleeper?

3. Do you toss and turn?

4. Do you snore?

5. Have you ever sleepwalked?

6. Have you ever fallen asleep in class?

7. How late do you stay up?

8. Do you ever have nightmares?

9. Why is it a bad idea to go to bed on a full stomach?

10. How many pillows do you use?

11. Do you wake up at the crack of dawn?

12. Are you an early bird or a night owl?

13. What is sleep apnea?

14. Have you ever pulled an all-nighter?

15. Do you ever talk in your sleep?

16. When was the last time you overslept?

17. What time do you set your alarm clock for?

18. Do you like to take naps?

19. Do you believe in the saying 'if you snooze, you lose.'?

20. What time do you get out of bed?

21. When you fly, do you usually sleep on the plane?

22. Do you have trouble falling asleep?

SOCIAL MEDIA

1. What social media do you use?

2. What's the most popular social media at the moment?

3. What's your favorite social media network?

4. How has social media changed the way we communicate?

5. What are the benefits of social media?

6. What are the drawbacks of social media?

7. Do you have to be on every social network?

8. What type of content should you share?

9. How often should you post?

10. How can you get more followers?

11. Do you really know all of your friends on Facebook and followers on Twitter or Instagram? Have you ever accepted a friend request from someone you don't know?

12. Which social media do you recommend for business?

13. How does social networking affect your privacy? Which bits of your personal information are publicly available?

14. How much time do you spend on social media?

15. How do social media affect your social life?

16. Are you addicted to social networking sites?

17. What is the future of social media?

18. How important is social media to your professional life?

19. How often do you take selfies?

20. When is it okay to like your own social media posts or photos?

21. Do social media affect our mental health?

STRESS

1. What are the causes of stress?

2. What are the signs of stress?

3. How do you deal with stress?

4. How do you wind down after a long day?

5. What are the effects of stress on the body?

6. What can you do to minimize stress?

7. Are you overworked?

8. Do you have a lot on your mind?

9. Can yoga relieve stress?

10. Can breathing techniques relieve stress?

11. How do you prevent a situation from getting too stressful?

12. Do deadlines stress you out?

13. Can you handle multiple tasks at the same time?

14. What diseases/illnesses can result from stress?

15. Is there such a thing as stress-free living?

16. What's the link between chronic stress and heart disease?

17. Would you consider taking a stress management class?

18. Do you have a lot on your plate?

19. Can stress be positive?

20. How can someone prevent burn out?

21. Are there any foods that help reduce stress?

22. Are you stressed out right now?

SURVIVAL

1. What should you do if you get lost in the woods?

2. What should you do if you get bitten by a snake?

3. What should you do if you are caught in an avalanche?

4. What should you do during an earthquake?

5. How does one prepare for a hurricane?

6. What does one do immediately after a hurricane?

7. What should you do to lower stress and keep a clear head in a survival situation?

8. What is a prepper?

9. What is a tornado?

10. What's the single most important thing you need to survive in the wild?

11. Do you know how to build a survival shelter?

12. What is a drought?

13. What's the difference between a hurricane, typhoon and cyclone?

14. How long can one survive without food?

15. How long can one survive without water?

16. Have you ever volunteered to help after a natural disaster?

17. Would you donate money to a natural disaster relief fund?

18. How would you survive as a castaway?

19. If you had to, could you live off the land?

20. Do you own a survival kit?

21. Can you start a fire without matches?

22. What does a lot of vegetation and swarms of insects often indicate?

TIME

1. Do you have the time?

2. Does time fly?

3. Do you go to nearby cities from time to time?

4. What time does your alarm clock go off?

5. At what time of day are you at your best?

6. Are you usually on time?

7. What's the difference between 'on time' and 'in time'?

8. How many times have you been to New York?

9. How much time do you spend on homework?

10. Do you schedule out your week in advance?

11. What time do you get off work?

12. What is the B-theory of time?

13. Do you live in the past, present or future?

14. Is time travel possible?

15. Would you rather have more time or money?

16. Do you wear a watch?

17. What time should you show up for a dinner party?

18. Is time the greatest riddle?

19. What is daylight savings time?

20. How much spare time do you have?

21. Are you having a good time?

22. What is rush hour?

TRADITIONS/CUSTOMS

What is the definition of *tradition*?

What traditions does your family celebrate?

How do you celebrate birthdays in your country?

What are some traditional dances from your country?

What are some summer traditions?

What are some winter traditions?

What are some traditional songs from your country?

What is traditional music from your country?

Is there a traditional instrument in your country?

Does your hometown have any special traditions?

What is some traditional food from your country?

Are there any school traditions, or classroom traditions that you practice in your country?

What are some traditional clothes from your country?

On what occasion would you wear traditional clothing?

Are there any foreign traditions that you admire?

Do young people know less about traditions than previous generations?

Do you follow any customs when going to a dinner party?

What are your traditional sports?

If you move to a new country, should you adopt their traditions?

Is there a tradition that you would like to start?

Is it important to follow traditions?

Should we create new traditions?

WEATHER

1. How you like this weather (we're having)?

2. Are you looking forward to the winter?

3. Do you get the winter blues?

4. What's your favorite season?

5. What's the weather like in your hometown?

6. Have you ever seen snow?

7. Have you ever had frostbite?

8. Have you ever gone skiing?

9. What is a blizzard?

10. Are you chilly?

11. Have you ever been caught in a shower?

12. What's the forecast for this weekend?

13. Would you rather live in Miami or Toronto?

14. Do you wake up at the crack of dawn?

15. Have you ever had frostbite?

16. Is learning English a breeze?

17. What did you do for spring break last year?

18. Would you rather live in a hot climate or a cold climate?

19. Explain the science behind global warming.

20. Is it overcast today?

21. Do you feel blue when it's gloomy?

22. Would you rather be very hot or very cold?

WEDDINGS

1. Where did you get married?

2. How many people came to your wedding?

3. How much does a wedding cost?

4. Who pays for the wedding?

5. Who hosts the bridal shower?

6. Did you hire a DJ at your wedding?

7. Was there an open bar?

8. What are some common venues for weddings?

9. Should you list a dress code on the invitation?

10. Who is the best man?

11. What are the duties of the bridesmaids?

12. Who lifts the bride's veil?

13. Is there an appropriate way to kiss at the ceremony?

14. What is the proper etiquette for the bouquet toss?

15. What is the proper wedding dance etiquette?

16. Who should make toasts?

17. What's the perfect wedding gift?

18. Do you have to stick to the gift registry?

19. How much should you spend on a wedding gift?

20. Do you invite your coworkers to your wedding?

21. Should the bride and groom send out thank you notes to everyone who attended and gave a gift?

22. What's the best wedding you have ever been to?

WORK/JOBS

1. What do you do?

2. What's the difference between a job and a career?

3. What's your dream job?

4. What time do you start work?

5. What time do you get off work?

6. Do you work overtime?

7. Do you get time and a half?

8. Do you get benefits?

9. Are there any perks to your job?

10. Do you get along with your coworkers?

11. Have you ever worked the graveyard shift?

12. Have you ever done shift work?

13. What's the hardest job in the world?

14. What's the most dangerous job in the world?

15. What are some prestigious jobs?

16. How do you get to work?

17. Is there any job which is beneath you?

18. What is an internship program?

19. Have you ever worked a double shift?

20. Have you ever worked the graveyard shift?

21. What's the difference between getting laid off and getting fired?

22. What is a blue-collar job? What is a white-collar job

WOULD YOU RATHER

1. Would you rather be here or be home?

2. Would you rather eat at home or eat out?

3. Would you rather live in the mountains or by the ocean?

4. Would you rather live in a place where it is always hot or always cold?

5. Would you rather your shirts be always two sizes too big or one size too small?

6. Would you rather have the ability to be invisible or be able to fly?

7. Would you rather give up taking a shower for one month or give up the Internet for one month?

8. Would you rather be rich and unknown or be middle-class and famous?

9. Would you rather speak two foreign languages very well or speak five languages not very well?

10. Would you rather be an amazing painter or an amazing musician?

11. Would you rather study French or English?

12. Would you rather go to bed early or late?

13. Would you rather eat French food or Italian food?

14. Would you rather be very intelligent and poor or not very intelligent and rich?

15. Would you rather be an MIT graduate or a Harvard graduate?

16. Would you rather work indoors or outdoors?

17. Would you rather stay home on a Friday night or go out?

18. Would you rather live in the country or the city?

19. Would you rather have a window seat or an aisle seat?

20. Would you rather eat junk food or healthy food?

WRITING

1. Do you like to write?

2. Have you ever written an essay?

3. What is a run-on sentence?

4. What is an opinion essay?

5. How do you write an introduction?

6. What is a sentence fragment?

7. What do you put in the conclusion?

8. Do you have good handwriting?

9. Can you read and write in cursive?

10. How many emails do you write in a day?

11. Is writing in English important for you?

12. Are you good at spelling?

13. How often do you write in English?

14. Have you ever written a research paper?

15. Does reading improve your ability to write?

16. Can you write in cursive?

17. How long does it take to write a book?

18. What are your strengths and weaknesses in writing?

19. How many words a minute can you type?

20. How many words should a novel be?

21. Would you like to write an autobiography?

22. Does writing require discipline?

Printed in Great Britain
by Amazon